THE MIDDLE PATH

By
D. A. M. BATCHELOR

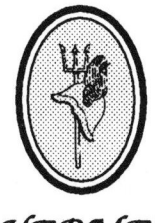

HERMES
2 Tavistock Chambers, Bloomsbury Way, London WC1A 2SE

ISBN 1 86032 000 7

Typesetting and cover design by Jim Barry

Made and printed in Great Britain by Booksprint, Bristol, England

FOREWORD

There are three things I would like to say in introducing this book.

Firstly, it is always helpful to a reader if an author makes it clear from the beginning what a book is about. This book certainly does. It is a book for people of religious faith, or of none, those who follow The Way and for those who are seeking to follow the Middle Way, the way that has no name, but IS.

Secondly, it is just as important to know something about the author herself.
She writes from the heart. She has been to the centre of her own existence, to the core of her own being. She has made the Journey inwards, as well as upwards, and found herself able to begin to restore, heal and love others through her own inner light and experience.
She has found her true Self. Within her heart there is as much space as there is in the whole world outside. She embraces both time and history.

Thirdly, Life is difficult - it causes pain - this is a great truth, indeed one of the greatest - but it can also be full of joy.
Dulcie has shown us how we can approach Life's journey, and above all she has shared with us her own enlightenment.

For this, as well as for much else, Dulcie, our thanks.

Ronald Dingwall June 1994

INTRODUCTION

The date, as I start to write, is 12th of March 1983.

I must begin by saying that for many years I have talked in my sleep. Many people talk in their sleep but this wasn't quite so simple; I talk in a Foreign Tongue.

My husband has heard me very often as it wakes him up. He will lay and listen to what I say and tell me about it the next morning. His usual words are "You were off again last night"!

The names Karaticus, Omer, Astarte, and Adomonte, came into these night time conversations and it seems I would say something, then wait as though waiting for an answer, and then I would start to talk again. For a long time this had no meaning to me.

I became intrigued by these names so I contacted a qualified hypnotist and he taught me self-hypnosis. My husband then questioned me while I was in a self-induced trance and counted me out at the end of the session. This was how, in 1981, the following regression tape was produced.

PART 1

CHAPTER 1

REGRESSION TAPE TRANSCRIPT

"Where are you? Where are you Dulcie?"
"Dark."

"What city?"
"No city."

"Are you in the Countryside?"
"Its Dark, dark."

"What are you doing."
"Sat ... sat waiting."

"What are you waiting for?"
"I'm trying to escape."

"Escape from where?"
"Escape ... Oh ... OH! (deep sigh)."

"Escape? Are you a prisoner?"
"Hole, big hole, ... big hole ... massive stones."

"Why are you in this hole?"
"I'm a prisoner ... of Caliph."

"Prisoner of who?"
"Caliph ... Caliph."

"Where are you then? Egypt?"

"I'm not sure, it is, ... it is not my home."

"You have been taken prisoner from somewhere, where were you when you were taken prisoner?"
"Korph, Korph."

"Korph! You are not in Egypt? Are you in Greece?"
[very deep sighs]

"Was it an island, an island? Sea?"
"Yes ... Oh yes! They came and took me prisoner from the temple where I served."

"From what Temple? what was the temple called?"
"The Temple of ... Corince, the temple of Corince ... "

[interrupting]
"Over there at Corince and brought you to -"
" ... Corince, ... its so dark!"

"They took you prisoner." [No answer]

"Where are you now?"
"They took me from serving in the Temple ... The Temple, for I served."

"Who did you serve?"
"I am the Daughter of the Goddess ... the goddess ASTARTE, but they ruined it, and they killed ... I can see it ... [moan]."

"Who are they?"
"The Traders, ... the traders, they smashed and killed and I tried to run ... I was running towards the steps running ... running ... but I never got there ... they caught me."

"Did they put you on a boat?"

"Yes, they caught me. I ... I must go on ... on."

"And where did they take you? Are you still on the boat?"

"No, ... No, big stones ... "

"You don't know where you are?"

"No ... No its dark only small!"

"How old are you?"

"About 23."

"23."

"I'm 23!"

"I want you to go forward a year, you are 24 years old, 24 years old. Where are you, where are you now?"

"I am IAH ... I am Iah from Corince."

"Corince? You are 24 years old, where are you now?"

"I will not obey ... I will not obey ... I am serving! Menial task, I am serving."

"Where, in Corince?"

"No."

"In Egypt?"

"It is ... my Masters are dark!!"

"Egyptians?"

"They are Narasaians ... Narasaians, they have large Temples but not ... but not to ASTARTE."

"Temples to who? Who are the Temples to? What Gods?"

"The Gods are not gods! Not Iah's God's"

"What Gods are they, do you know what they call them?"
"They are, are peculiar ... peculiar!"

"Can you describe them?"
"Yes, Yes they are frightening! Oh, Oh."

"Are you frightened?"

"Ah yes ... they are not nice, not nice they make Iah feel bad,
I pray to Adonis."

"Lets go forward now, you are twenty eight years old, twenty
eight, where are you?"
"I GOT AWAY."

"You got away?"
"I am Back!"

"Back where?"
"I am back in Corince."

"You are back in Corince, at the Temple?"
"I am back, I am back, I am there."

"Has it changed?"
"Yes."

"It's different?"
"Ruins ... Ruins!"

"Ruins? What year is it, do you know?"
"It is, it is 14."

"What year is it?"
"14 ... 00."
"14 and two zeroes?"
"Yes Yes."

"What are you doing at the temple?"
"I tried to live ... I tried to ... But!"

"Where do you live?"
"I live in a small cave."

"In a small cave. Are you alone?"
"I'm alone."

"Have you no friends?"
"No, no friends, can ... cannot trust anymore."

"How do you eat?"
"I go to the orchard, to ... to."

"To the Orchard?"
"I drink the milk of the she goat. I am sure I will be all right."

"I want you to go forward in time now, go forward. You are thirty five years old, thirty five years old, where are you?"
"I have my Brother."

"Who is your Brother?"
"KARATICUS is my Brother!"

"Where did you find him?"
"I didn't find him! He called me, called me."

"He called you from where?"

13

"From beyond the Beyond."

"How did he call you?"
"He Called!"

"And did you go to meet him?"
"No, NO."

"How did you meet him?"
"We meet ... we meet in the Twilight Zone .... twilight zone."

"Was this in Corince?"
"NO, this is everywhere."

"It was everywhere? ... And what did you say to him when you met?"
"I was so glad as I could not endure much more. He tells me I must go on. I must go on!"

"Go on doing what?"
"I must not give way to anything but to serve as I promised. To serve as I promised ASTARTE!"

"Is your brother going to take you with him?"
"My Brother, my brother is in the twilight zone, he waits in the Twilight Zone."

"Are you in the Twilight Zone?"
"No, NO"

"You are among the Living?"
"The twilight is living!"

"Is it?"

"All is Living."

"How do you go into the Twilight Zone?"
"I walk into the twilight zone, and meet my Brother. He reminds me of my vows."

"What does he tell you?"
"He tells me my vows and that I must keep them."

"What are your vows?"
"My ... my vows are to serve ASTARTE all the days of my life."

"To serve who? ASTARTE?"
"Yes, ASTARTE."

"Where is ASTARTE?"
"ASTARTE is the Mother Goddess. ASTARTE is the Mother."

"I want you to go forward in time. You are now forty two years old, forty two years old. Where are you?"
"I am in Corince."

"You are still in Corince. Have they rebuilt the temple?"
"NO ... NO."

"What are you doing?"
"I'm just passing the time, they took it all. I am waiting."

"What are you waiting for?"

"I am ... I am waiting because there is so much to be released forever. The Council say it is Time! Karaticus says it will not be long, but I must abide. I must try hard to abide."

15

"I want you to go forward ten years. Ten years have passed you are fifty two years old, fifty two years old. Where are you?"
"I am so tired, so tired."

"Are you still in Corince?"
"Yes, but I have friends."

"Who are your friends?"
"There are Tiffa and Omer. They bring me fruit ... and I teach them ... teach them about ASTARTE."

"They do not know ASTARTE?"
"I tell them."

"And what about your Brother?"
"He is in the Twilight zone, Karaticus is still in the twilight zone."

"Do you speak to him often?"
"Yes, but it is more difficult, for I am near to Completion."

"I want you to go forward in time. You are sixty three years old. You are sixty three years old. Where are you?"
"I CAN SEE THE SEA!"

"You are still in Corince?"
"I can see the sea. I have moved ... I have moved. I have gone to the cave."

"You have gone to the cave?"
"Oh yes, OH YES. I have gone to the Cave, I am HOME, I AM HOME. I am on the coast line. I'm in BASA ... BASA!"

"You are where?"

16

"BASA ... BASA."

"Is it in Corince?"
"No, NO I'm Home. It is on the coast line. I had to go to the cave."

"Why did you go to the cave? Why did you have to go?"

"They called me, I was called."

"You were called. Who called you?"
"They did ... THEY DID."

"Who are THEY?"
"They are those dressed in ... those in!"

"How many of them?"
"There are five."

"Five men?"
"Yes. But they are five. They called me to seal the SEAL for all Time."

"Can you describe them? What seal would it be?"
"To be SEALED, to be Sealed through all LIFE as a witness in all things. It is difficult! But it is a Seal on Earth and flesh. A SEAL in all dimensions and zones."

"Go forward in time. You are now sixty eight years old. Go forward. You are sixty eight years old. Where are you?"
"At sixty eight years old I was still receiving the SEAL."

"Go forward in time. Go forward, you are seventy years old, seventy years old. Where are you? Are you in the cave by the

Sea? Are you in CORINCE? Where are you?"

"I am very ..."

"You are an old Woman, you are old?"

"I'm old?"

"Where are you now?"

"I am no longer sure. My eyes are dim, so dim, it is DARK."

"I am going to bring you back now to the present time, to the year 1981. I shall count from five to one and you will awake.

FIVE, FOUR, THREE, TWO, ONE; AWAKE!"

CHAPTER 2

IAH

It is not easy to listen to this regression tape and understand it after all these years but I am going to try and do my best. I sent this tape to Mr Peter Moss who, with Mr Joe Keaton, wrote a book called "Encounters with the Past." He sent me the tape they had made while researching their book so that I could compare it with mine to see how genuine my tape sounded.

One day, it became so clear it was as if I was being told. Karaticus and Omer; that was what I called out in my sleep, and they were both on the regression tape, so was ASTARTE! It was as if I had brought them through from my sub-conscious to my conscious state and they became real characters to me.

I have raised six children. All of them are grown and two are married. I have 5 grandchildren. So I am well aware of what life is all about. I am now over 61 years old and a Spiritual Healer.

After making the tape we went to Crete on holiday. On a tour we were taken to the "Palace of Knosses" and we came upon what was left of a flight of steps. I stopped at the first step and I was so frightened I could feel my heart thumping I was so scared. It was as though I was frozen to the spot. I was afraid and called to my husband to help me because I couldn't move even though I was only a few inches from flat ground. As we left I felt I could hear Iah saying "I was running, running towards the steps!" The next place we visited was a beach. As we stepped onto the beach I noticed that, there on the right hand side of the beach, a lot of caves were set up in a cliff. I said to my husband "I know that cave! That Cave has an altar in it." We went straight across the beach and up to the Cave I had pointed at. All the way there I kept saying I'd lay my life on there being an Altar in it and there was one! It was the only one with an Altar, but it wasn't just that. It was the feeling it gave me that this was the cave used by Iah.

Again I could hear IAH saying "I'm in a cave, Tiffa and Omer are my friends." I didn't want to leave. This cave had no beds in it; all the other caves had stone slab beds which suggested that, at one time, they had been lived in. But this cave seemed to have been put aside as a place of worship. I tried to find the History of the caves but all I found was that the early Christians had used them, and that was long after the days of IAH. I was in for a few surprises when it all started to come together but I knew there was something. If I said the name Karaticus to myself, something stirred deep within me; and as I said ASTARTE to myself I felt humble! So I went on trying to find some answers.

Since making the tape and these bouts of talking in my sleep in a Foreign Tongue, I have tried to check on a few of the statements I have made on the tape. I found this most interesting. In 1400BC the Minoan Civilisation seemed to break up and disappear. Knosses was in Ruins. Was I at Knosses for some reason? Had I gone from Korph to be at some religious Ceremony? Who were the Traders? Were these the steps I fled down? I have only been frightened by two flights of steps in this lifetime. The first time was at the steps of a church in Cornwall when I was four. The second time was, while in Crete, when we went to visit a Turkish Fort. I got as far as the Entrance. That did it; wild horses wouldn't have dragged me into that fort. I felt like it was just one awful place!

But how did IAH now her time was 1400 years before Christ? Is this knowledge gained in a later Incarnation?

When my husband asked me what I ate I said, "I go to the orchard," I have checked this. The Island at one time grew all the fruit trees known in Europe.

There are some things we do not understand in our every day life but we just accept they are there, just as I did when the next piece of the jigsaw slipped into place. In Crete there are many Greek churches but only one Cathedral, its name is "To Our Lady Of The Cave". This really made me wonder. Iah said "I'm Home." Where was she? In a cave? It's what happened in this cave, she was called to "seal the seal for all time." For all time; I repeat it as it is in this lifetime that what this Seal is all about has become perfectly clear.

Sometimes things come to us in a flash of insight. We may meet someone for the first time but we are quite sure we know this person. Then we get the opposite feeling, we feel our hair stand on end and really dislike someone we have just been introduced to. Well this is caused by the vibrations we give off, but from where? They are from the soul. Genesis describes the soul as the body plus the spirit and this is the definition I always use even though it is quite common today to use the term "soul" to mean just the undying part of a person, i.e. the spirit.

There is much more to life than one incarnation, it is just too wonderful a thing to be born only to live a few years, then die and have to wait for the day of Judgment. Rubbish, of course it is not like that. I can tell you most truly that you are not born only to die and then sit in some place twiddling your thumbs for, perhaps, million of years.

I believe the following is what happened and I am going to bring proof from this lifetime! Long ago I lived in Crete, my name was "IAH" and the goddess I worshipped was ASTARTE.

21

The Middle Path

My spiritual brother was Karaticus and, this is the important part, I received the Seal for all time as IAH to be used in all dimensions and zones (Earth And Beyond).

As Iah I had taken certain Vows, including one to serve my Goddess all my Life. Today we have nuns, and monks and many Orders that take Vows. Many people dedicate their lives to a purpose, so this is nothing new. What I want to do is take you back to a time before Jesus Christ. It does annoy me so much when people will call people of those times Pagans, or Heathens.

Who are we to call them such. They worshipped according to their time and beliefs. They used God's Names of that period but God is God no matter what you call him. They were no different from today - each man to his own Creed. If we take a look at the Holy Bible it states, "I went into them by my rightful name, Jehovah, and they knew me not." Its like a man named William, but who is always called Bill. William answers to the name Bill but he is still William. In the same way, God also answers to other names. He knows that all his children, all over this Earth have their own pet name for him. Don't forget that he has been around a lot longer than man and he knows us better than we know ourselves.

Let us think back to the time of a Mother Goddess who played her part among the Gods. Why a Mother Goddess? Well, Man saw that the earth gave of its food and seeded for the next crop. He saw that it was the woman who gave life or seeded the next generation. He worshipped the Earth as it was his life support and he saw that Woman was also the support of new life so she became as a "GODDESS."
Now let us take a look at today. Woman is still worshipped in the Church today (so we should watch who we call Pagan). The

Virgin Mary is worshipped as "The Mother of God, the Lord Jesus Christ." If we go back in time, Rhea was the mother of Zeus, so the pattern of worship has not altered really. It is only modern man up to his old tricks of saying that we are so much wiser than the ancients! I can accept without any problem that I was Iah and that I served ASTARTE, the Goddess of Venus, and if I look at it in its correct context, the Virgin Mary is worshipped and served with the same respect today.

CHAPTER 3

THE TWILIGHT ZONE

Now I would like to take a look at the Twilight Zone that Iah went into, to meet her Brother. What is the Twilight Zone? On the tape I am asked if it is the land of the dead and I reply, with strong conviction, that it is not. I say it is living and that all things are living. Then I am asked how I get into the Twilight Zone and reply "I walk into the Twilight Zone." In the Old Testament one of the prophets states "and I saw in a night vision." What is a night vision? Well, we dream at night when we sleep particularly, for me, when I am half asleep, half awake. A Prophet would dream, then tell what he had seen or had been told to reveal. The Twilight Zone is the same place as the night vision given to the prophet. I believe most sincerely that we can receive instructions on life while we sleep and I will prove this to you when we come to talk about the lifetime I now live.

We see with our Earthly eyes, we sense with the nose, etc. But what about the wind that can cause such damage, rip off roof tops, pick up and throw a thing for miles. Can you see the wind? You may see a form it takes, like a whirlwind of dust, but that's only a form. There are many things we know exist but cannot see. We cannot see the Air we breathe but without it we are dead. The Twilight Zone is just like that, unseen but it is there.

A good Medium can most certainly pick up and tune in to the next dimension, the reason this is done is not only to give a comfort to the distressed but to confirm to us all that Life is continuous. Other dimensions also exist but, like the Twilight Zone, cannot be seen by Earthly eyes. There are seven dimensions from the lower to the higher.

The Middle Path

I am going back a few years, twelve to be exact, when this twilight experience happened but there is no last year or yesterday for me, time it seems is all one.

Again I was half asleep half awake, it seems to me that this is the way these experiences come. Maybe it is this way that the sub-conscious part of the spirit communicates with the conscious part. I recall that I was stood on the edge of a cliff, and that it was very beautiful. The colours were brilliant and just below, in a pool of water, were the most colourful fish you have ever seen, swimming and flipping, tipping and turning. All of a sudden, I knew I was not on my own. Someone was standing beside me and I turned and looked up. He had nothing on his feet and was wearing a loose white gown. As I looked up, I felt I was in the presence of a very Holy Being. He gave me a feeling of utter peace. He looked at me and said "You have a long path to tread, it is not going to be easy but you can do it. The path is covered with brambles and prickles, these are the problems and troubles you will find as you go through life, push them away, hack them down as you would brambles, don't be afraid, no-one can harm the Real You."

It is not by having faith in God alone that helps us. We must have faith in ourselves as well. God helps those that help themselves. We pray in faith but our Prayers may not always be answered to our liking but God is not going to give to one of us anything which is not to our advantage. We are here on the path of progression and some of us are having a very hard time right now. All that we see around us was foretold many years ago.

In the Holy Scriptures we are told there is but one Path. Of course there is, that is the very Path you are walking upon. Many Religions will tell you that only they have the Truth. This is not so, the truth is that which satisfies your inner self. There are many classes in this school of learning, each with their own Teachings and Knowledge but no-one has the ultimate truth.

CHAPTER 4

The Regression tape stopped before the death of Iah, so I do not know end of that lifetime, but I am very aware of the beginning of this life.

When I was born into this Lifetime I was born with a birth mark right in the middle of my forehead. It is still visible, all the more so "When I am about my Heavenly Fathers' Business." My mother was very disturbed about this mark and took me to the family doctor. He told her that there was no way it could be removed. She asked him what it was and was told its an 'anathema' which is also known as a "Mark of Nemesis." Not to be put off she took me next to the Wise Old Woman of the Village who told her "Before you drink anything in the morning, lick the birthmark with your tongue. The poison on your tongue will kill it." But all the licking didn't kill it! I can always remember that I wore a fringe to hide the birthmark. I'm now 53 years old and it still shines like a beacon at times. The Book of Revelations by John says "Touch not the earth until I have Sealed my servants in their foreheads." Do you think that I presume too much? When we get onto the life I now live you will think differently. As I do the work I am called to do, this birth mark stands out for all to see. Do I still carry the mark of the SEAL that "IAH" received in the days of "ASTARTE?" YES - I Believe I Do! Did I take Vows in those far-off days that I would Serve the Purpose of the Middle Path and on each reincarnation, life after life, that I would serve God, for all time? It would make you wonder, if you were me. The birthmark is there and so are the Scriptures and so is this lifetime's work. I try in many ways and I hope I will be always as aware as Iah was of the Vows and that I will Honour them always as she did.

I was born into this time on the 19th of August 1929. My mother and father were in service and as ridiculous as it may seem when she was six months pregnant with me she thought she was putting on weight so she went to see the doctor. He soon told her why. I was well on the way! This caused great confusion in their lives as they had no home to go to. My mother was a cook and my father a valet. My mother worked to the day I was born. I was born at Taunton in Somerset. It made my father's day as I was born on his birthday. We used to laugh together as I was born at Five to Ten and he was born at Five to Eleven. A very special love would develop between us that death only strengthened.

I was taken to my Grandmother's home, in Devon, by my Mum and Dad and we lived with them for the first twelve months of my life. As I have explained I was born with a birthmark. I believe my mother was a very superstitious woman and it did bother her. She had lived in a small village in Devon most of her life where, even now, a lot of the old ways are practised. At one year old I left my Grandmothers home when my mother and father moved into a little Lodge on a nearby estate. My father was a Forester and mum was a Gate Keeper, she had to open the park gates for the Lord and Lady of the Manor when they came down from the Big House in their car.

I have had many psychic experiences; they started while we were living at this Lodge.

For four more years I was an only child. The lodge stood on its own so I had to amuse myself. In the park was a chestnut tree. It had a lovely low branch and I used to sit on this branch and swing for ages. I loved that tree, it was my favourite pastime. I must have been under five when this happened as I cannot recall my brother who was born when I was five years old. On this day I went to the Chestnut tree and was swinging. Suddenly this thought came to me, "Next time I will be a singer." Then I saw, as though I was looking at a film screen, three separate things that were going to happen to me in my lifetime. I can recall this as though it were only yesterday, as though it had just happened. Two of these things came to pass and caused me a lot of pain and suffering from the age of nineteen to twenty-six years old when I really bit the dust. But looking back over those years I realise it made me question life and it also taught me a darn good lesson; that as I sowed so I would reap. I hope I have managed to pay off any debts I owed, for I would not like to face those experiences again. The third thing I saw was the old people trying to put their hands up to their faces, they were very frightened. Why? Because they were being attacked by Young Children. Let us remember I was not yet Five years old when I saw this. It was unheard of in 1934 for children to attack the elderly but what about today? It is all too common and sad that many of our old are really afraid of our young ones. Karaticus has told me since that I was allowed to see these things so that I was prepared for what was to come in the future and the work I had taken on to do.

I went on through life, my Grandmother was a great one, when I started school in her village. I loved to sit with her by her large coal fire in the winter. She would poke the fire with her poker and say "Can you see the pictures in the fire? Tell Gran what you can see." I could see the Pictures and I would tell her, and she would say "that's a good girl." Little did I know she was encouraging me to use second sight, to use a part of me that was to have such a good effect on other people in my latter life. I do recall one time when I wasn't so keen on Gran. I used to have the most terrible Chilblains. I went in one day and they were itching like mad. "Come here to me" she said, "I'll cure those things." She put something on my fingers and held them to the fire. "Oh! the pain" I cried, it was murder but I have never had another chilblain in my life.

At the Lodge where I lived I slept in the back bedroom. I recall so clearly now I would be semi-asleep and I would slip out of my body, float up to the ceiling and fly around. I would look down at myself in bed, at my body asleep. I did this many times. Also, a ball of light would come into the room and travel around between the ceiling and the top of the wall. Later in life I often wondered if the person who wrote "Peter Pan" had these flying experiences.

My life went on, like us all I made mistakes, bad mistakes that I paid for dearly but it taught me, they say that nothing comes cheap that is worth having. I would get very strong moments of knowing that something would happen and I would think, that has happened before. Or did I dream it? Once I went to Ealing and I knew as we turned the corner what was coming. It was exactly as I had seen it in my mind. I was young and I suppose because I was used to these things it didn't bother me. In fact I could easily have thought they happened to everyone. Like I have said before, from the ages of Nineteen to twenty-six, life was a real nightmare. Several times I said "Why me God?"

CHAPTER 5

SEARCH FOR A LOST SISTER

I want to go back to almost four years ago to 1979. My
husband's mother had died when he was eleven years old
leaving six girls and two boys. One of the girls, Marguerite, had
been adopted at the age of three and over the years my husband
had often said he wished he knew where she was. This day, and
I know it was a Sunday as a family had found a lost relative and
it was in the Sunday paper he said, yet again, that he wished he
knew where his sister was. It was like another part of me "came
alive." I could feel it rising inside me: and I said "I'll find her
for you." I thought "What have I said? Whatever made me say
that?" Yet something inside me was saying its okay, calm
down, everything is all right. I had committed myself to a
seemingly impossible task but something inside me was saying
'it is all right.'

The Fates, (I call them that but it is more like a pattern we come
to work out), play a large part in our lives from time to time. We
had just been to visit my sister-in-law in Plymouth and just as
we were leaving she gave her Father's old deed box to one of
my sons. Several days later I thought about what might be in the
box so I looked through it. There was his old driving licence,
a few old photographs and some personal papers but right at the
bottom were two letters; two very important letters. They were
from the lady who had adopted Marguerite and on another
scrap of paper was the telephone number of the London
Adoption Society. I had found my first little bit of evidence.
Having the name and address of the adoptive parents I was able
to apply for her certificate and I was fortunate, I received it. I
remember only too well the day it came. I had not been feeling
too good with the flu and it had put me to bed for a couple of

days. One morning the post arrived and my husband brought me up a letter, I opened it and called out "It's here - the certificate for Marguerite, its here!" Now I was getting somewhere I thought, but I was in for a shock. I had it all right, all the names were correct - fine - until I read the following note at the bottom of the certificate: "Readopted!" I looked at it again. It couldn't be! Have you ever felt your heart go down into your boots? Mine did, I felt that I was not going to find her. I felt deflated. Then, a calmness came over me and I felt the inner me say: 'Hang on.' Then it came to me; the scrap of paper with the telephone number. I rang it and my luck was in. A nice old lady answered and I explained to her how I came to be looking for Marguerite. She told me she could recall that the little girl had been sent into a Home as the marriage had broken up. She kindly gave me an address that had been the brother of the woman who had adopted her but I had no luck there. What next, I thought.

The Salvation Army were so kind and good; and they did their very best but they could find no lead to where she had gone. Then, thanks be to God, the Fates stepped in. One night I went to bed as usual, I was half asleep, half awake, when suddenly I saw my friend Sally who had passed away about two years previously. Sally and I had been such good friends and she was sadly missed. As she stood in front of me she had such a calming effect upon me. She came towards me smiling and I recall so well saying to her. "Hello Sally." Behind her I could see another figure and I said. "Who have you got with you Sally?"

Now, I have only seen photographs of my mother-in-law. Both Marguerite and I were only three years old when she passed away. The shadow came forward and I could see her as though she were in the flesh! It was my long deceased mother-in law and as she came closer I called her by name "Grace, Oh Grace" She tried to speak and seemed to find it difficult. Then she said quite clearly "Horton Cross, Horton Cross. Regilded the Clock! Regilded the Church Clock." She looked at me with such love in her eyes that I felt I wanted to cry, then they both seemed to fade away. My husband and I searched maps of the greater part of England and we just could not find it, but it was there as we discovered later.

We lived in Leicester at this time and we were on a visit to my father in Devon. Suddenly a small sign post caught my eye - Horton Cross! It was a small village in Somerset. As I went through that village I felt like I was being drawn out of the car. It was as though something was dragging me. I went very cold and white, which bothered my husband so he kept saying "Are you sure you're all right?" I knew inside me that something was at Horton Cross, I was picking up something! I was sure I was reacting to something. We stayed in Devon a few days and decided to go back to Leicester the same way we had driven down which meant going through Horton Cross again. This time the feeling was very strong and I was sure I was right. It held a clue to Marguerite's whereabouts. I said to my husband that the next time we went to Devon I wanted to visit the Church in Horton Cross to see if they had regilded the clock. Time passed and we prepared once more to visit my father. As we neared Somerset I felt a great anticipation, in fact my knees were knocking! The village came into sight and I felt a lot calmer. The Church was on the main road so we stopped. I remember getting out of the car. I looked up but there was no Clock? I walked towards the church door and it was as though someone had their hand on my back and was pushing me.

'Go on, Go on,' a voice was saying to me. I walked in and saw a lady cleaning. "What am I going to say?" I thought.

Again the great feeling of "It is going to be all right" came over me. I spoke to her and told her I had come to the Church for a very special reason, I explained how I was looking for my Husband's sister and then told her how I had been given Horton Cross and that the Church Clock had been regilded. She said "Oh my dear, that's two miles down the road in the next village!" I went very still inside. "Do you know?" she said "they only put that clock back up last week." I was lost for words. I knew my sister-in-law was very near. How often does a Church Clock get regilded? If I had come to that Church when we had first gone through Horton Cross, the lady would not have been able to tell me as it had been at least six months before when we had passed through and she could very well not have been in the church. To go through these kind of experiences makes you realise that there is no doubt that life is continuous, and the saying that there is "more in heaven and earth then meets the eye" is true.

One night, I had the most terrible nightmare you could wish for, I was half awake, half asleep again. It was as though some terrible force was trying to force me backwards, as if I was trying to walk against a gale force wind. I was crying "Marguerite, Marguerite" It was very dark and I went towards this place, it seemed to be a house with a light in the passageway. There was a nurse inside and I said to her "Where is Marguerite?". She said "She is in the Birthday Room". I tried to get through and it was awful, it was a terrible place. They seemed to be biting and scratching each other. Several tried to grab me and one stuck a silver pencil in my leg. I felt it go in. I was so terrified, and then I saw her.

"Marguerite, Marguerite" I was screaming "come here quickly!". I am not a Roman Catholic by Faith but I called out "Mary Mother of God, protect me, Michael the Archangel

36

protect me." As I came back to my awake state, I was sweating as though I had fought a battle. Some time later I found my sister-in-law, she had been adopted twice and married twice but with help of those who dwell in the Twilight Zone and the undying love of my mother-in-law I found her. Let me explain to you where she was. On leaving Horton Cross you go through St Marys (Mary Mother of God protect me) to the next village which is St Michaels (Michael the Archangel protect me). And in the very next village was my sister-in-law. She has the same size family as myself and, incredible as it may seem, has a caravan in Devon one mile from my father's home. When we first met I felt very strongly that I knew her, there was something, it wasn't the first time our paths have crossed. I shall never forget her words to me "Dulcie I have always wanted a brother and you have given me a real brother, it's wonderful" My brother Karaticus says it is wrong to let this experience not be explained. "Love is the strongest emotion, it can be felt and passed through all dimensions."

What happened was all planned by the time Marguerite and I were conceived in the flesh. We quote the scriptures "There is a time to be born and a time to die". The plan was that we would rely on the teaching that "Love overcomes all things". My Mother-in-law was in one Zone, and Marguerite and I on the Earth with the Veil between us. Marguerite waited patiently for me to find her via the love of her mother. It was a plan that was fulfilled. One last remark on this, my sister-in-law had been missing for fifty years, and you might like to hear what happened at Horton Cross just after I found her. My new found brother-in-law had a car accident right outside the Church! This experience taught me a great deal, Karaticus has explained the pact we took part in. It showed me without doubt that life exists at all levels. All we do when we leave this earth is to change levels. Love is everlasting, it does not know the meaning of birth and death. I am talking of real love, not physical attraction.

CHAPTER 6

BECOMING AWARE

While I was looking for my sister-in-law I was given the address of a very well known Medium. I wrote to her and asked if she could give me any help in any way. I got quite a shock when her reply came. Nothing much to help in my search for my Sister-in-law but she said "You are a natural born Healer, and you should be using it." That gave me something to think about. A short time after this I was fetching my son from school. We were half way home when a little old man, who was tottering towards us, almost fell and I caught him quickly. As we were outside the Police Station, I said to my son "Quick go into the Station and get help, get one of the Policemen to help Mum." I thought the man was drunk but I couldn't leave him on the pavement. The poor old fellow said "No! No, don't do that; just let me hold on to you a moment and I will be all right." I suddenly realised that I could not smell drink on him so I hung on to him. In a short while he seemed to be all right. I asked him where he lived and he told me. I said "Come on, its near my home." As we walked along he said "You don't know me, but I'm a Medium. I have helped Ena Sharples," and he mentioned quite a few other well-known people! When we came to parting he said "I want you to take back what you so readily gave me." He put his hands upon my shoulders and I felt a power go through me and I recognised how it felt.

"They have given you one hell of a time in the flesh, but they cannot touch your Spirit for you are clothed in Purple," he said. I left him and made my way home. I told my husband when he came home from work what had happened. He asked if I had ever seen him before and I told him "Never." I was to meet him again though. A couple of weeks later, there he was as large as life on the front of the Evening Paper. He had told his neighbours that he was going to win a television in a competition and he had! It stated he was a Medium and, like he had told me, he had many famous clients. In the back of my mind began to stir again what the Medium had written to me; "You are a Natural Born Healer." The little old Man had said "Let me hold on to you and I will be all right." As I left him he had said "Take back what you gave me so," and I had felt so good.

On one of our holidays in Devon we went to see my aunt and uncle, who lived only a few doors from my parent's home. My uncle had been sick for quite some time. I had always loved to sit and talk to him as he could tell good stories. He had started work at a very early age, and had been one of the lads who had 'put his age on' and "run away to sea" to join the Royal Navy. He had served his twenty five years service when war broke out but he went back for another four years. He'd seen a lot of action. It seemed so wrong to see him sat back in his chair looking so under the weather. I gave him a big hug and made a fuss of him. I told him I would be back later to see him and went down to my mother's house. About an hour later the door opened and in came my aunt, looking agog. I asked what was wrong and she said. "I've come down to find out what you did to your uncle." As I looked at her, I could see she was really happy so I knew everything was just fine. "I couldn't believe my eyes" she said to my mother, "he hasn't been out of the house for weeks. Dulcie comes up to see him and when she went he calmly says he wants his boots because he's going to the garden for an hour! You wouldn't think there was anything wrong with him" To me it was my final proof; I had the gift of healing! I promised myself that day I would use it wisely, and do all I could to encourage people that this power came from God. As Jesus said; "all things you have seen me do you can do also."

CHAPTER 7

MOTHER

After we had moved to Leicester we had brought my parents up from Devon on holiday, they had really enjoyed it as most of their lives there had been no holidays. My mother had a lovely time as big stores were a dream come true to her. I remember with happiness how she would find something she needed just to get into the city. That was all very well, it was getting her to leave that was the problem and in one of my daughters, Marguerite, she had the greatest friend. Off they would go and you could be sure they would not be back until after the shops had closed. It was the traffic that worried me as mother expected the cars to stop and let her cross the road. Not for one moment did she think that it was far safer to wait and cross by the lights.

Sometime after this I had an urgent phone-call "Come home quickly, Mum is in hospital and they say she hasn't got long to live." I caught the first train I could and raced to Devon. I went with my sister-inlaw to the hospital and I recall so well how she was laid in the bed looking lost and forlorn. My mother had always been such a happy-go-lucky person. I went over to her and said. "Come on Daisy-Bell, no good lying down in the bed like that." I asked my sister-in-law to give me a hand and we propped her up. As my hands touched her I knew it was time once more to use my god-given gift. It is very wrong in my mind to make a show of this gift because it is simply a matter of being tuned to receive this cosmic power and passing it through to the person needing it. So I just held her hand, and smoothed them, and prayed from inside myself. "If it be Thy will Father, please let my mother be made well." In no time the voice inside me said, "All is going to be well." I went to leave and as I did I said to her, "I want you to be good and eat your supper when they bring it round." She smiled and said "I'm tired." We went back in the evening and there she was; sat up in bed. Her first words to me were. "I've eat me supper Del" I felt a lump rise in my throat, and once more I thanked God for the gift he had given me. The hospital had said there was no chance for her but she made it and even came up to Leicester twice after that. About two years later we were taking her back to Devon after she had been up to stay for a month. I noticed she had been quiet the last few days and had insisted on giving one of my daughters her engagement ring. All the way home she didn't have much to say for herself and when I left her I didn't feel too happy. She had only been back in Devon a few days and she was back in hospital. A few weeks later came the telephone-call. "Come quickly, its mother."

Luckily for me my husband could take me by car. As soon as I saw her I knew there would be no healing this time. She was in a semi-conscious state and didn't really know anyone. I went back into the hospital the next morning. I looked at her and I felt the "Inner Me" start to come to the surface and it had a message "Get ready to work." So I let that part of me right through and I called. "Daisy-bell, Daisy-bell, its me, Del." She had always called me Del, not my full name, unless she was really mad with me over something I had done. "Now if you know it's me just tap once with your finger on the palm of my hand. Tap once if it's "yes" and twice if you want to say "no." Listen, it's Del. do you know its Del?" As big an effort as it was for her, her finger raised up and gave one tap. She knew it was me. I knew she may not be able to speak to me but we had not lost contact. I could talk to her and knew she could hear me. On the fourth day, I noticed a change in her and I knew as I stood there that time was running out. I recall I said "Dear God please give me the courage to go the last half mile." I felt the Spirit descend upon me and a feeling of "Do thy Duty that is best, leave unto the Lord the rest!" Picking up her hand I placed her fingers on the palm of my hand and said "It's me, Del. Do you know it's me?" One feeble tap.

I started to talk to her and I could hear myself saying to her "Can you see a light?" Two taps. "No", I said "In a very short time you will feel that you are in a passage. At the very end of it you will see a strong light, will you go toward this for me? I promise you that you will be quite safe. Will you do this for me?" Her finger tapped once. I felt such a sense of relief, I can even say I felt happy. My Duty was complete.

My father had not been well that morning so I went back to him and made him have a light lunch. Then both my husband and he fell asleep in their chairs. I thought I'd go up to my brother's home which was only a short distance away. I play the piano a little and I asked if I could play theirs. I hadn't played for years.

My mother used to be so pleased as I could just about manage to play their favourite song "I'll walk beside you." My sister-in-law said of course I could and went upstairs. I sat down to the piano and before I knew it I was playing "I'll walk beside you". A feeling came stealing over me; I can only describe it as utter peace. I felt free; a great lightness came over me as though something had been lifted. Suddenly the telephone rang. As I went to the phone I knew what had caused my feelings.

"This is the hospital" said the voice on the other end of the line "Your mother has just passed away." Mother had walked down that dark passage and into the light. I called my sister-in-law, "Mum's gone." Her reply was "Who is going to tell Daddy?" "I will of course. I will tell Dad," I said. We walked down the road to his house, I dreaded this moment that was before me.

43

The Middle Path

As I have told you we had such a close relationship He was still asleep when we got there but I knew I had to wake him up, I just couldn't put it off. So I woke him. I remember I knelt down on the floor beside him and I looked up at this man I loved so deeply. "Daddy, Dad, Mum's gone." He looked at me and said. "That's why my head has been so bad all morning." I know I started to cry and he said "Come on Maid, we still have each other," I felt sad but those words registered with me and I felt so safe. He and I belonged together somehow, it was like we had always been close. I was to find, in part, the answer to this feeling of belonging.

CHAPTER 8

FATHER

My father was a quiet man, a man of few words, he never expressed any religious views. When I told him about my healing he said. "You are just like your Grandmother, use it for all the good you can do Maid."

He never talked about her other than to say she was the local midwife and a good friend to her neighbours. My father was in the World but not of the World.

After my mother passed away we would go down to Devon as often as possible to see Dad and every year he would come up for a six week holiday. He managed very well on his own and every Sunday he would go to his son's home for lunch. I used to laugh as he said "I get a good blow-out up there" He had a great love of ice cream and my brother used to say you just couldn't give him too much, there was no such thing as "too much" where ice cream was concerned.

We had asked him to come and live with us but he said "When I can't manage anymore on my own then I'll come"

How true those words were going to be.

I wrote to him in May 1982 telling him. "Pack up your kit bag and I'll be down on the 27th of June to fetch you".

When we arrived he seemed to have the "shakes" terribly and I asked my brother how long he had been like this. He replied "He's never been like this before." He seemed to settle down and I put it down to the fact that it was a bit of tension coming out as he was always glad to see the car roll up to the door as he hated the motorway; in fact we used to use the old Roman road when we had to go back with him. Something wasn't quite right though; I could sense it but the feeling passed away.

I pulled his leg by saying I hoped he had his bag packed because we were going to turn around and go straight back to Leicester. "Suits me" he said "I'm ready," and he was. We left the next day and he slept most of the way in the car. Now, sometimes a thing does not register with us until sometime after it has happened. Outside my father's house ran a brook and in the summer if there was a thunderstorm, it would overflow its banks. So each year we would have the job of laying sandbags inside the front door to keep out the water. This time he didn't bother, he just locked the door and got in the car as though he was thankful 27th June was here at last. For a man of 81 years he had a good memory so it was strange that he had apparently forgotten to do it this time. When we got home he couldn't get into the house quickly enough. His case was up the stairs and he was soon in fine fettle, sat in his chair. My husband had taken a week off work and we took him to Derby Tram museum which went down very well. We took several other such trips but I began to notice he was getting tired after the slightest exertion. I started to think he would not be with me for much longer and that we'd better make the most of it. On the Monday my husband returned to work and Dad got ready to collect his pension. He was gone some time so I went to look for him. I saw him coming towards me and I knew then that he would never be going back to Devon. I realised that this was why he had had the shakes when we fetched him; he knew as well and he had worried that something would stop me bringing him to my home; the shaking had been relief. I walked towards him "Dad, you've been gone an awful long time, come on, lets go home and brew the pot." "Yes Maid," he said "I'm so tired." I took him to bed and called the doctor, who came the next day and gave dad a good examination. He came down the stairs from dad's room and I told him that I knew Dad was in a bad way; that I knew he was going to die. "You're right" said the doctor, "he has two massive tumours. But how did you know it was so near?" I told the doctor that I just knew. When my father died he was full of cancer. It wasn't easy looking after him knowing he was so ill and I believe my father knew this so he decided to make it easier for me. One day he said to me "Maid, I'm going home" That was his way of saying he was going to die and I said "I know." Well" he said "in my case you will find all you need."

He had even brought his birth certificate. He had not forgotten to shore up the front door; he *had* known all along that he would not be returning to Devon. Life was a little easier after that as we had both accepted the fact. I would sit for hours with him. He had very little pain.

I couldn't give him a new body but with my Healing I could ease the pain. The doctor was so kind to my Dad. He couldn't understand why Dad wasn't in more pain but I knew why and my Dad knew why, and that was all that mattered. My father suddenly found his tongue and he told me all he had kept back over the years, and how dear I had always been to him. All he could think of was that if he could be with "his Maid" he would be all right and I promised him I would look after him. As you will notice he always called me Maid! One day we were talking and I asked him why they called me "Dulcie" "Oh I didn't want to call you Dulcie" he replied, "I wanted to call you Vinalia" It was like someone had thrown a bucket of ice cold water over me. The name Vinalia rang a bell somewhere in me.

He looked at me very deeply and said "Maid, you and I are two of a kind." I had to get away from him as I felt as though my heart was going to break wide open. I went downstairs and all I could hear in my head was "VINALIA," over and over again.

I found a reference book and tried to find it. I was looking at VENUS and I saw it; VINALIA, a festival to Venus, celebrated on the 19th August. Both my father and I were born on this day but that is not all; Astarte, Iah's Goddess is the Goddess of Venus! Who was my father? Where had he found that name? He was not an educated man, but he knew that our birthday fell on the date of a festival dedicated to Venus. And he wanted to call me Vinalia after the name of the festival.

A few days before he passed away I sat on his bed and he suddenly smiled and waved his hand. I said to him "What's up, Dad." He said
"Our Lanty is here, and there is our Alice."
He spoke to them quite rationally and then he looked at me and said "They have gone back and closed the door."
He was talking about a brother and sister-in-law who had passed away several years before. I told him not to fret and he replied "Oh yes, they told me it's not quite time yet." Right to the end my father was very clear in mind and in control of his body; he never even soiled the bed. My eldest son, who he loved very much, came the day before he passed away. He stayed and talked to him. I was up in the bedroom with them. My son asked Dad if he was all right. He looked at him with the naughtiest of smiles and said "Boy! I got a good bed, and the best maid servant. What more can a man ask for at the end of his days?"

Then he slept. The next morning he was a lot less with me, and very restless so I asked if anything was wrong. He said it was the door, he said it wouldn't open. Suddenly I realised it was the door he had seen his brother and sister go through.

He asked if I could open it for him. "No" I replied, "but I will pray for help and when the door opens I want you to slip through." His eyes shone with light and he said "I'm going on but I will keep a place at the Table for you Maid." I kissed him Goodbye and he slept away. The Doctor came and confirmed his death. He came downstairs and said "Your father died a happy man, but I can't understand why he has not had to have any form of drug to ease the pain, he had two tumours." I didn't say but I knew. I had been able to repay my father just a little of what I had owed him by using my Gift of Healing for one whom I had loved so very dearly. I have, since my father passed away, had definite proof that he is still in existence. My Father will come to me now and then; I can hear his voice very clear in my left ear saying "I'm here Maid."

PART TWO

I believe that there is no beginning or end. When the holy bible states "I, the Lord God, will visit the sins of the fathers upon the third and fourth generation of them that hate me," it is not our great-great-grand children in the Flesh but we, ourselves. The bible states clearly that the Lord God is a just god! Would a Just God punish you today for the sins of your great granddad? Of course not; that is not Justice. What we get a rough time for is the mistakes we made in a previous life and that is what being "Just" means. As we have sown so must we reap, of this I am quite sure. It is not God's fault if we are greedy, selfish, liars and cheats. We are the ones that do these things, not God. If we can't follow a lot of good advice we were given then we deserve the consequences. We were offered good guidance, a set of rules to keep us on the right road. Did we take it? Not on your life, so please don't blame our Father in Heaven; we alone are at fault. The commandments were the best help you could have wished for! If you break the Earthly laws you get punished, so it is with the Heavenly laws - well, if we ask for it we must expect it. As I have said, "God is Just." It is we who are unjust. It is Man in incarnation, ignoring the Laws set by God, that is the biggest enemy to himself. As long as we go in the way that we are we will not pull ourselves up towards the light. As I say this I am told that I am to complete the experiences of this lifetime and than we, Karaticus and I, will try to do what we are called to do. He says that first, we must let you know how sincere we are in trying to help you all, and that the part I am playing in this lifetime will put the whole plan of working together through reincarnation before you as a very true fact.

Look, I will show you something very clear. Both the Roman Catholic and the Protestant churches say Jesus Christ is our Lord and Saviour. Then they go out and shoot each other or

51

blow each other to bits! How dare they assume to call themselves followers of Christ! He taught that it was wrong to take each other's lives, wrong to commit murder. It is wrong for one simple reason. Each soul comes to this earth to increase its understanding. To progress so that one day he can come off the wheel of reincarnation and take his rightful place back in his Spiritual Father's Home; call it heaven if you want. If a man's life is taken before its time, if he is murdered, then that Spirit has to come back to the earth and start again. This is why the commandment was given; "Thou shall not kill. The scriptures say "he who slays by the Sword shall die by the sword". It may not happen for a few life times but that is what is meant when I say we have a just God. Do you see what is meant by "as you sow so shall you reap!" You come to this earth so many times.

As man, away from God, is blind to Reason and Purpose, he believes he has only to please himself and in our times it is very evident that we have gone too far with today's terrible weapons. If peace was called by the whole earth tomorrow what is going to happen to all the stockpiles of these destroying agencies? You can not bury them for all time nor expect them to just go away, out of sight out of mind doesn't work! This is Man at his worst, all he is concerned with is the moment. Each leading country on the Earth wants supreme power, they forget future generations. All this has happened before and like the rebellious Souls we will not accept the advice that the Bible, or the Vedas and many other Holy scriptures give us. We much prefer to think we are more intelligent than the men of the past who wrote these books yet it is ourselves that we are denying in a past incarnation! That is how unintelligent we are. When Christ was upon the Earth he said "I do not come to bring Peace among you" Why? We, and I have been told to state we, which is my brother Karaticus and I, are going to try and help you to walk up the Middle Path with us.

52

There have been many more experiences in my life. I have worked with the help of my faithful brother Karaticus and, under his guidance, have been able to help many people. I do not have to look for them; a path is opened up and our paths cross. My brother and I are what are referred to on the Earth as Twin Souls. This has nothing to do with the flesh, it is to do with the spirit. Just as we have twins in the flesh, so we have twins in the spirit.

There have been times when we have worked opposite to how we work today, and times when we have both been in incarnation at the same time. We both belong to the same group of spirits that have progressed at the same rate.

It is to be made clear here, so that we start off on the right foot, that a soul is formed when the spirit and flesh are joined in incarnation. As all the scriptures state that the body without the spirit is dead. So, at death, the spirit finally leaves the body.

There have been a great many teachers sent all over this World in every Era since this Planet became a "school of learning". Two thousand years ago a great teacher came to Earth called Jesus Christ. Some call him the only begotten Son Of God but the Vedic scriptures also describe a virgin birth.

Jesus came under the title "Saviour." Well there have been many "Saviours", Noah, Moses and many others, came to try and help Man understand that he is that he is not just flesh and bones.

I do not want you to get the impression that Jesus Christ came to deny any form of scripture; he did not, he came to fulfil it. God has talked to all men all over this Earth. This is why the apostles were told to take the message Christ had brought to the

Earth so that for once, all men everywhere would have the same Message and to put it quite simply the message was "This is the last round up." 2000 Earth years are but a twinkling of an eye in Time Eternal, so don't run away with the idea that God has overlooked his promise to cleanse this Earth. All the given signs are with us but perhaps we are too taken up with our own lives to see what is right under our noses!

In recent years we have put satellites up into our skies. The scriptures say " and strange things will be seen in the sky!" Its an eon of time ago, I can tell you that anything like a satellite took off from this Earth. We have had strange Visitors in their own kind of transport but they didn't come from this Earth.

We have had wars and rumours of wars for a long time. The old Testament says "Son shall rise against Father, Mother against Daughter. Neighbour against neighbour." Well, we have on our hands all this so the Prophecy is still on line. It's all happening to us.

Are our children not disobedient; take a look at the papers. Young children beating up old people! And much more. You don't need it spelt out for you; it is right in front of us. No-one wants to take a lead in trying to get them to see their folly. We, and those before us, are all to blame. Life has got so cheap it has no meaning to all but a precious few who get sat-on if they try to rise in protest. We hear that God is Dead. Christ is torn to shreds by those who are born in ignorance. I wonder if their books will be in circulation in 2000 years time? I don't think so, but his Teachings are! Its a great pity that Man has always interfered with the written word and I'm afraid that this is what has happened so often with scripture. You only have to change a comma to make a sentence sound different. Let me show you an example.

"Verily I say unto you this day, you will be with me in Paradise"

Now let's move the comma.

"Verily I say unto you, this day you will be with me in Paradise"

This gives two very different meanings. In the first sentence the speaker is saying that at some unspecified time in the future we will be together in Paradise. In the second sentence todays the day! You can see how a slight change of emphasis, by moving only one comma, it is possible alter the whole meaning.

This is only a small example to you of what has been a right mess up of the Bible. Many other errors have been introduced during translations from older languages to modern languages.

You may ask why reincarnation isn't mentioned in the Bible more openly. It is, they didn't manage to turn it all around to suit their "hell and damnation" theme as well as they thought. You see, for many years, Man has been led into fearing God more than loving him. Why? For the simple reason it made the churches rich and powerful; and truly, as Karaticus has just said, "In their Skirts are the blood of the innocent Sinners."

Man was so scared of the fire and brimstone they preached that he went hungry to pay for churches to be built. I believe that in Malta that sometimes there is a church at one end of the village and another at the other end. Nowhere in the Scriptures will you find God ask Man to build such places in such abundance.

What better could the Church do than to make Man believe there was but one chance, so out went any leaning towards reincarnation in the Bible. Let us have a look at an example that has survived.

The Lord, talking to Job, said "Before I formed thee in the belly I knew thee! Tell me if you can remember."

So where was Job? He was in existence because God could remember him.

Jesus Christ taught "Unless you be born again, born of the water and the Spirit, you cannot enter the Kingdom."

Man is born through water, he lies in his mother's womb in a bag of water. He enters the World through this water when it breaks. His body has a high water content. His Spirit is what enters the body of flesh because he needs to have a covering of the same material of the World into which it is Incarnating. No matter what World we Incarnate into we need a body of what that School of Learning is composed of. Just as when we have finished school and go home for a break we leave our uniform behind, when we die we leave the body of flesh behind where it belongs. It is stated that flesh and blood can not enter the Kingdom of heaven. This is because it is of a different composition.

A man can live for weeks without food but without water he dies very quickly. Water is the key word. What Christ was saying is he must be reborn, and seeing this statement was given to Man of this Earth. Water being so important to Man's very existence Christ tried to show us we must come back here, and be reborn. It is very easy to understand. Let us suppose this message was being given to a World whose main life stay was *acid*, then it would have been said "unless you be born of the acid and the Spirit!" Sounds funny to you does it?

When Jesus Christ was about to leave the earth he stated "I go to prepare a place for you, for in my Father's House are many mansions." Today these "mansions" would be called "Dimensions." Yes! That is what it means for there are many levels of growth. If we look around us, here upon the earth, we have so many different types of people, all with different ideas, temperaments and values. Each person living according to what he is. Have you ever stood beside someone and felt you had to move, that you cannot stand the feeling coming from that person. Then, at another time, you get completely the opposite feeling towards a stranger you meet on a bus, start to talk to them and feel like you've known them a lifetime? Here you have examples of why, in our Father's house, there are many mansions. When we go back home, for a rest period, what better can we have than to be with those "the stranger we met on the bus". On the Earth we have a saying "Like draws Like" that's what our Father's House is like, like draws like. A natural law draws us to where we belong, or rather the dimension we have earned for ourselves, so that everyone is at a state of peace.

It is when we get on the Earth we hit the problem as we are once more all in the same barrel, which is made worse by the increasing population density of the Earth. It is like St. Paul when he says "Now I see through a glass darkly" or, to put it into modern words, to see through to the other World is like looking through smoked glass. It is faith that God asks of us, "faith in all things." We are told to believe in all things until we prove them otherwise. That is very good advice as this is how Man Progresses. Just stop a moment. Take a look around you. Look in the mirror, take a good look! *Who are you? Why* are you?

See the eyes that give you sight. Look at your tongue! Could be it has many uses but why? Look at your hands, feel how they grip. I will go no further, but to ask you most seriously why you feel you are You? My friends, you are too wonderful to be any form of nature's accidents.

Think about it. Let your mind clear for a moment. Now, let us see it as it really is. Look at a tree in winter, can you picture it? It looks dead doesn't it? Spring is on its way, can you see the bud, look closely now! Summer is just around the corner, tiny apples are forming from the blossom. Autumn now and you can go and pick those tasty apples. They taste good don't they? Do you notice how it all follows a pattern? First the bud from something that looked dead. Then the leaf comes to shade the fruit that appears in summer, and in autumn the fruit is ready to pick and eat. From that example we can each of us see ourselves. We are born (bud) then we are children (blossom). We grow up, and have children of our own (apples). In old age we mature and reach the Autumn of our life time, and like the Apple, we are picked, but we are picked from the Earth. What do we *taste* like? Sweet or sour? An acid or in-between *apple?*

It will all depend on ourselves and how we handle Life. What we have got to try for is to taste of all that life has deal out to us. We should except that we are here to learn, not to turn bitter when life gets tough but to pray for guidance. I promise you if you will only have a little faith and believe that God knows you, as he knew Job, you will get help to see you through a bad spot but please don't forget when things are going good to be thankful also. It works both ways. Long, long ago this Earth was set aside as a School of Learning and Man has never been deserted by God. Would you desert your children if you saw them getting into trouble? Of course you wouldn't. God is not dead, it is just that we have lost our way a little and need to take a look at the advice Our Father gave us in the first place. Now we cannot go back to the real beginning of this time as the Bible states Adam and Eve where told to *"replenish"* the Earth, which means to refill it but we will go into that at a later time. Let us take a look of what is left of the story of "Moses." I say this because I feel that the Bible no longer contains the full story; we should remember that many books, perhaps as many as 12-14, were lost during the many translations of the Bible.

Moses was a very high Incarnating being, it has always been in the plan that when Man needs a leader, a Teacher has been called from the Sixth Dimension, the Highest being the Seventh. The Lord God was having one of his usual problems with Man in the flesh. So in the council it was decided a teacher would lead man back into being a little more orderly. It has always been the same, and I will tell you why. Man gets "God" muddled up; He either has got him up so high he is out of reach and beyond understanding, or, he has Him so low he can't find Him. But neither is correct, if you will come along the Middle path you can really get to know Him, and listen to the good advice He gives you. That's what it is all about really. A father advising his children. What was behind the Lord God's idea to have Moses take a group of people for forty years into no-man's land? This group of chosen people were so called as they were cut off from the rest of Mankind to be *re-educated*, on how to live in incarnation in this life and what was expected of them. The reason why they were taken for forty years is very clear; there would be a new generation at the end of it. A child of two taken in would be forty-two on reaching the new lands, and would have children of their own. A teaching would be well established by this time. The Lord God said "Come up here in the quiet of the mountain and we will get "The rules of life ", in their correct order, written down for them." "Here is the first commandment" said the Lord God. "Thou shalt love the Lord Thy God with all thy heart, with all thy soul and with all thy mind."

How does God want his children to love him? With the Heart (Physical), Soul (Spirit in incarnation) and mind (intelligence). So we are to love him with our complete being, no cheating, not

59

just playing lip service, but all the time. Why? because he is the Lord God, co-creator of our whole being as it was he who created the Man of clay. As the Heavenly Father is the Father of the "Spirit of Jesus Christ," so he is the Father of our "Spiritual bodies."

The second commandment is "Thou Shalt Love Thy Neighbour As Thy Self." Don't tell me this is not possible! Everything is possible if only all would get together and try. Its been done in small groups, so it could be done by nations if only they wouldnt be so Power-Mad. These two commandments are the greatest according to Jesus Christ. If these two could be lived we would have no need of any others.

Do you think the "Lord God" is asking too much of us when he asks us to love him so completely. Stop a moment, don't you hope to gain on this Earth this kind of love for yourself? From a Son or Daughter, or your husband or wife. So why shouldn't he ask it of us? We have a great weakness in the flesh; we feel others can do it but we can't. Trouble is, we get the wrong idea of love. Moses, as you may know, had a lot of problems with his group of people. He wasn't up in the mountain for five minutes when they had melted down all their Gold and fashioned a calf. See, Man must have something he can see with his eyes to worship. It seems you cannot get through to Man that God is not interested in Idols of any kind but is intent only of our returning to his home.

How did the Lord God appear to Moses? He spoke to him as a man speaks to his brother, face to face. God's hands covered Moses to protect him from the glory of God but Moses saw the back of God and he seemed to Moses to be a man. See what I mean when I said before that Man has put God so out of reach with his Ideas. We are created "In the Image of God" says Genesis (I and 2). Wherever apeman got his ideas from that

God, the Lord God, was something our minds couldn't grasp is just out. Jeremiah says *"Behold I have seen God and live."* And the promise is "That you shall become as Gods." Also when Jesus Christ appeared to his apostles in his resurrected body and ate fish, etc, it was still in the image of a man except the atom was different and he could split the Earthly Atom and walk through walls and it was in the same body that he was gathered up into the clouds. Where is the mystery of what God looks like? If only we could step back in time we would see that history has repeated itself time and time again. We are in one very bad time right now. Underwater archaeology is proving this. They are finding walls and pavements which had been on dry land at one time. Great Civilisations have been on this earth, we have played many parts, in our life times upon this earth.

The problem man has on the earth is that he cannot seem to bring to a balance the working together of spirit body, flesh body and mind. What is the mind? It is intelligence. I'm quite sure that this serves both bodies. The human brain is a wonderful part of Man. It beats me how anyone can believe this ever evolved out of nothing. But it is the evolution of the spirit that is important; not our bodies.

We get an awful lot of genetic mix-ups; this was caused years and years ago by the very fact that certain tribes were told not to intermarry and of course they did and caused a genetic problem. God then created a division of tongues among Man to keep the races apart but Man continues to ignore the advice given at the time of the Creation.

As I have said before, God in all times has spoken through the Prophets chosen men, but man will always go his own way, and never thinks that life catches up with him in the end, and I can assure you it does. You cannot sow without reaping. Isn't it fair, when someone causes you terrible mental cruelty that they should get a taste of it? This is what God meant when he said "An eye for an eye and a tooth for a tooth." We do not hand justice out; God does, so no one gets away with anything. So wouldn't it be easier for us all if we really took a good look at the advice he gives us. It would you know. The Soul of Man is about to go into a new age, the age of Aquarius which will be an age of peace that follows Armageddon. Jesus warned that Armageddon would occur as the Earth became more peaceful. This happening now with the emergence of organisations like the United Nations but the new age is still many years away.

It is not the body of man that is altering, it is the Spirit that is going to receive more enlightenment, and is going to take this massive leap forward. So we have to prepare ourselves, we cannot take this step as we are, for the Souls are too caught up in the dense Earth, and have to pull away from the idea that everything is based on this Materialistic World. Our technology is great, so was that of other very ancient civilisations. Don't forget Sodom and Gomorrah. Let us remember the Prophecy made by Jesus Christ, "As it was in the days of Noah, so shall it be in the last Days." Why is it we cannot accept these things? We have proof that the Earth was flooded at one time, each country has its stories of a great flood. Why do we suppose it can't happen to us? Over our heads hangs a threat of war, so wicked in its outcome, it is driving Man to a state of thinking "what the hell does it matter; tomorrow I die". Not so, that is just what the opposing power wants you to believe. The real you cannot die; it can be badly shaken up but it is of a different material than your earthly body and cannot be destroyed. Like I have said we are not far from the time of Cleansing that is to come to the Earth. That is why so many souls are reincarnating and we are a little overcrowded. It is one of the finest times for a Soul to come to the Earth for testing. We leave the Spirit Home full of hope; its when we get here and become pulled into the system we go off course. It in one of the best times for the Soul and Intelligences, to get together to overcome the temptations of the Earth. Most of the things we fall for only line another man's pocket with money and, to be fair, the children today are coming into what previous generations have built for them. You cannot put on some of those television shows without affecting their conception of life. It is not like when I was young and went to the pictures once in a blue moon if I was lucky. They are watching TV every day of the week.

The Television companies are there to make Money, they are not worried if they brainwash the children into thinking that TV is a way of life. So you see Man is sealing his own destiny, he is going into it right up to his neck. Why? because its big Money, the biggest enemy of God, and doesn't the Devil know it, and he is aiding and abetting all those who have forgotten their purpose in life. Take a look at the world, everything hangs on sex. It was given to Man to Procreate, to produce more bodies for reincarnating Souls. I don't need to say what a mess its been made into. They teach the children in School, if you teach a child any thing its going to practise it, we have more problems over sex than you know how, let me remind you that so did the people at the time of Moses and Noah. Man cannot evolve without making mistakes, that's why it takes so many Life Times to even get started. But, this is for the best because the harder it is, the more you will learn. If you will but make a sincere effort then God is there to give you a hand. Man gets lost on the way, this is why the Cleansing is on its way. We have made it hell on earth and its got to go back once more to square one. Many of you will say "Yes, Thank God," for you are very sick, inside of yourselves, to see Man degrading himself so. We have come on stage for the last Act, make no mistake about that, you and I have been on stage many times, we take part in this Play many times, playing different roles, the same as any actor plays but we are here to improve our Talents not waste them. Each time this School Of Learning is geared up to go into action, and the Play is about to start its run, the Producer, and Director, who are the gods, have given us good advice, but do we want to listen to them? Oh no! What do we say? We will play it our way. And so the Play becomes a flop, and off the stage we have to come with our tails between our legs, and we have to go into Rehearsal all over again. We get some Leading Actors come in the form of both men and woman and they try very hard to get us to listen to the advice of the Producer and Director. "Look" they will say, "if you will only try to stick to a bit of advice on acting your part you will do fine." Do we? oh no! The Ego of Men says "I'll play it my way, I don't need you telling me," and so we fail, like all Earthly plays fail if you get a lot of knowalls on stage. The Earth is proving more and more of what I am telling you. Skulls, that are thousands of years old, have been found with holes caused by brain surgery yet they were supposed to be primitive man.

They found a silver cube deep inside a Russian mine. I don't now the date of that one but it was from far in the past. "Out of the Earth shall come the truth," that is what the scriptures say, and the truth is that Man has been on this Earth one awful long time. Do you think this Earth cannot come into disaster over a moment in time, it can and has, and will. It seems that man reaches a peak in "the Play" and its swish and the curtains come down. We all know of the great empires but they do not last. Why? because each time we have such greed, selfishness, hate, anger - all this trouble arises as soon as Men get a little power and it goes to their heads and then its stand-by - "What I say goes." If only he would have a little sense and stop and think about how he could benefit other peoples lives, not how he can rule their lives then we could all get somewhere. Our problem is this we cannot seem to get the body, spirit and mind to work

64

together and yet it is possible for we have the example of the Holy Trinity. Here it is shown how a Triple-unity worked as one, when do we see times like these? As bad as it is, I believe War unites a country. Why? because everyone becomes a part of a whole. Neighbour cares about neighbour and there is less "I'm all right Jack". It should be more "Are you OK chum?" And I feel sad that Man is far more inclined to Pray in these times. I wonder if the Lord God says 'they are at it again down there, the lads on the Prayer are busy.' No, I'm not trying to be funny because it happens to be the truth. It's so easy to talk to God, he only wants you to talk to him in your everyday way. Lots of 'thees' and 'thous' are not needed. When I'm under pressure I do and talk as much as possible then I say "Please Lord, give me a hand up. I'm in trouble," and my prayers are answered. Sometimes the answer comes into my head like a flash. Other times, the situation I'm in doesn't seem half as bad as that of someone who crosses my path with a much harder one. It makes me realise just how fortunate I am. Too often we make our own lives a misery by just not being glad for what we have. Its this lifetime your living, make the most of it. Do your best with what you have got. Don't look up the scale with envy, you will only cause yourself misery. Look below yourself and say "there but for the grace of God walk I." This is a good thing to remember.

Karaticus says that all promises that God has ever made to Man he has kept. I picked this up from him as I was thinking abut the prophets. He tells me that man does not always have to act out a religious role when he is called by God to serve the "Middle Path."

There are many called to show the way by simple kindness. There are a thousand different ways men is called to the path set by the Gods. You should never, never look down on anyone, you cannot afford to do so for that person may be of high incarnation come to serve in a special way.

The Middle Path

The tramp in the street may be here to test not only himself but also those who walk past him and cock their noses in the air.

Who is to say if it won't be for you to live your next life as a social outcast. Don't forget what they did to Christ. Man, through ignorance, can be very cruel. It seems that Man has this knack of kicking a dog when it is down. I believe he does this out of fear that it could be him.

Jesus Christ promised he would send us "Prophets and teachers." Joseph Smith was very much like "Moses," he was called and he gathered a group of people together. It is most interesting how these people survived because although they went through some very hard times they stuck together like glue through all the trials and hate against the Church. The Church has now grown and has a very large following. But you see even here they had problems with Man in the flesh. Gods' Law of Consecration, which states that each person should have their fair share, was set in motion but could it be lived? No, so instead of putting in all to be shared fairly the Law of Tithing had to take its place. The Law of Tithing states that everyone provides 10% of their goods to the Church, who will then share it out. Man is forever changing. Joseph Smith's last words were "Don't worry they can't kill us." They did in the flesh but he knew they couldn't kill his spirit. What is so interesting about Joseph is that he said "If I was to tell you who I really was (in the Spirit) you wouldn't believe me." Yes, he Knew his true identity. But like Christ promised, they killed him. Teachers come in all walks of life, not only in the Churches, in fact it is more likely they will be on the outside of a church. Why? Most have come up through a path of a set sect and found it did not answer many of the questions they asked so they have had to go inwards into themselves to find the answers, remembering that God said "To thy own self be true." Its no good to you if you are looking to

66

a sect for answers and they don't add up. It is very simple to ask your spirit to bring up the answers if you are sincere in your seeking and need help to get a better grip on life. You start by putting the earthly cares out of your mind. Sit and relax, from the top of the head and work down to the tips of your toes. This is the hardest part but you tell yourself "I am in full control of myself and only I am the controller." I personally say a prayer of protection asking that the Lord Jesus will protect me while I seek myself, I relax , and dwell one the question I have. Sometimes my inner self has got the answer already, then at another time I could be peeling potatoes and, bang, the answer comes. I get a great deal out of this because I know my soul giving me what God told me I have and that is "The Truth is within me" - and that truth is satisfying to the Earthly me.

I want to touch on the way many of the young are trying to find answers through drugs, what they are doing is really of no use because not only are they getting a false picture, as the psyche rejects forced or abused use, its not that part of yourself which is tuned in God the Father. If you are not very careful the only thing you are doing is to line some one's pockets and get a habit you will have an awful job to drop. Its far easier to let yourself relax than to stick a needle in your arm or take a pill. What is more you get what you are looking for and that's not a load of colours or the screaming ad-dabs!

I am, it seems, to sort out the statement I made about the two creations.

Genesis Chapter 1 describes one creation, in this the animals are created before Man. God said "Let *us* make man in our own image." Everything else had been created. So there was to start with more than one God! They created both male and female and they were told to replenish (to refill) the Earth.

Genesis Chapter 2 describes another creation in which Man is created before the animals. Verses 2 to 4 state very clearly that it was the Lord God who was concerned with this creation. Plus the fact that it had all been created before it was in the Earth now again it points out to us the importance of water. It says very clearly for the Lord God had not caused it to rain upon the Earth. No woman was created you will see in the second creation, as in the first, but she was created from Adam's Rib (Genetic). The Lord God was the creator of our earthly bodies of clay, but it was from the home of our Spiritual Fathers our bodies of spirit came from, to incarnate into the body of clay of the second creation.

If you will take a good look at John 2(1) you will see that Jesus Christ is called The Word and it states that all things were created by him, and he became flesh. This is why when he and Satan met up on Earth they had been opposing powers, in a long drawn-out battle for Mans soul when on Earth.

Satan is the opposite power to "the Gods." You cannot have Positive without Negative. If there was no opposing power it would have been too easy. It seems the Spirit of Man comes into its own with far more determination if it is under pressure, one example of this is during a war. Also with the opposing power entering the scene we have a choice, we please ourselves what we believe. No one says "look these are the rules and you must stick to them."

When Adam and Eve (Genesis Chapter 2) were created from Earthly material and she partook of The Tree of Knowledge, it states "and their eyes were opened." Now it would be stupid to think they had been walking around with their eyes closed. This, you will see, is what happened. Their Spirits had entered their Material bodies and they had become "Souls" but up to the time of Eve taking knowledge they, like a "Seer" had been seeing with their Spiritual eyes. Now this is interesting, before the "fall" they had no children and yet they had been told to procreate. Why? because for the simple reason their bodies were not quite ready. As I have said "there is no positive without negative." The Gods waited for the negative to enter the scene which it did in the form of Satan, playing Ventriloquist, through a snake. But let us take it one step at a time so that we see it clearly. "Their eyes were open and they saw that they were naked." Why the panic? It is very clear that they were not used to this situation. In the body of the spirit they must have had some form of covering otherwise the last thing they would have been was ashamed. It is clear from scriptures that Satan was at one time a "Son of God." He was allowed to walk between the Heavens and Earth. Well he was a type of being that liked to think he was always right, very handsome as he is likened to precious jewels he always has had the swagger and poise of a "get out of the way, I'm here," type! He had been told quite straight by the Council of Gods to keep to his rightful place. Satan wasn't having that so, its very simple, he changed sides. In other words he "jumped the wall." When the Lord God called Adam and Eve and they didn't show up, it was clear to him something was wrong, when he caught up with them one look at the aprons of fig leaves was enough. "Quick, remove the tree of everlasting life or the whole plan is going to blow up, as it is we are now going to have a plan of redemption."

You see, even the Gods have problems! Now that Adam and Eve were really "In the flesh" they began to procreate, and Adam had a son in his own image just as we are created in God's image.

You see it's no good closing your eyes to the fact that a fall and redemption plan may have been used many times by the "Gods" and its a part of a programme. Please don't forget that

69

Adam and Eve did not only replenish this Earth but were also responsible for the Creation of the new born spirit world in Genesis Chapter 1. All creation is circular and this is why it is everlasting, without beginning or end.

The thing we have to keep in mind is that we are very much a part of the Programme and its to our advantage to stick to the rules. Every time one of us falls on our face while in incarnation its setting us back, each one of us, Black, yellow, red and white; the colour of our skins is not a guide to what is in their hearts and minds. Take a look at this.

Not how did he die but how did he live, Not what did he have but what did he give?

Those few lines sum it all up for me. How do we live these days? We live in fear, that's how. True, the prophesies are coming into full action, but, we need to know more than ever who we are and why we are here.

Can you really image that you could learn enough in one lifetime to become as Gods. That is the promise of the scriptures! Can we not see that this idea only came into being to keep man in fear of damnation as preached by the churches believing that they could keep the contributions coming, and keep Man in line. No one of this Earth can keep another man in line, and does the Lord God not ask us to love him with all our being? How can we love someone we feel is going to send us to damnation if we make a mistake? The churches contradict themselves very often. Jesus Christ, and may others from the past, have come to show us a very simple way of life and that is to do our best in each incarnation to be very aware of not only of yourself but those who travel with us. We are all of one big Spiritual Family. The only stipulation God ever laid down was that against intermarriage between certain tribes. There is wisdom in that for each carries its own lessons in incarnation and as it comes time for us to learn the lesson this Tribe gives, we are born into it. The earth in its present state is having one really bad time but, as we have sown so we must reap. If you have no respect for another man's feelings then why should you expect respect from others. It all starts with our selves.

It is so stupid to say that if a man isn't a Christian then you believe him to be an unbeliever. That man may have ten times the faith we have and be a far better person than us. It is simple really, the man is on that path he chose to be born into, or was advised to take by those with far greater knowledge than we have. Is it so hard to understand that we are only one tenth aware. If we were fully aware our Earthly mind would blow apart but let us remember, that although we have a part of the brain that is not used, we may well be coming up to a time when it is going to be used and that this is the next step in Mans evolution. This part might be nothing to do with the thinking mind at all but a part that is going to evolve to help Man see his part in the Whole Performance rather than just in one of the Acts in which he partakes, and leaves the Stage temporarily to reappear in a later Act.

We are, it appears, in a time of darkness. For example, the churches are seeing the congregations getting smaller! Why? because the Message, of what is all about, is not getting across. But new leaders are going to teach and help the people to find themselves because this is the whole problem. Man has lost his identity and is running around blind. All times that have been on this Earth have had periods like this, they come at intervals when they are due and the Power of Darkness creeps over the Earth. At these times, God's messengers come into action. The Reason to be born and die are the first things taught. Then comes the advice on how to overcome the Darkness we are going through. The Earth as we know it today will undergo great upheaval, lands on the surface will go beneath new seas. What of the reincarnating Spirits? some will be finished with Earthly incarnations but those who are not will either reincarnate on other Worlds or stay in the Spirit world until the new Earth is ready. The spirits who have progressed as far as is possible in this school of learning may choose to go on or to come back as teachers once the new Earth is ready. But at each clean up of the Earth there has always been a remnant left of it that was not destroyed. I will show you two examples from previous times. The scripture reads "and there were giants in the earth in those days, men of old reknown," men left from the time of a previous cleansing. We have Men and Woman on the Earth who still carry that Genetic coding. Lets have a look at Dwarfs. Fairy Tales? not on your life. They are no fairy tale. They also have their genetic coding going. We still have the little people so you see at each "clean-up" a certain amount of life is preserved, but please note this very carefully, they are as we are just larger or smaller, so each time the creation of the Earthly Body sticks to the same Pattern. In the Image Of God he created them male and female.

That "There is nothing new under the sun" is a very old saying. This is the truth, Man cannot discover anything that has not been discovered before, sometimes to the great advantage of Man. Very often he will discover a wonderful thing but it is to what purpose he puts it to that is the problem. If only he could see that things are given for our benefit and we could discourage the lust for Power of Man over Man we would have come up the Middle Path so much better, but the opposing powers of God have got into the position and this is our own fault that most of our great discoveries have been turned to destruction.
Karaticus says we should say a very simple truth, "Man is born onto the Earth and lives maybe seventy years and he is so sure

that by the time he leaves it he 'Knows it all.' He says the problem is that we allow our minds to dwell too much on what the "Experts" say. If only we would go into ourselves, by simple meditation, we would find that most experts are only well read men! To truly understand himself each man should find "Himself" for the knowledge and Learning of each lifetime is stored in the subconscious. He tells me that when the cleansing is over, each living soul will judge themselves by their own records. Hence the scripture says "judge not lest you judge yourself." We are very fond of judging others, it is so much easier to see their faults and guilt than to take a good look at ourselves and say "You have made one hell of a mess of that." He tells me we are one of many progressing families, way out beyond Man's wildest dreams in Space there are many Earths, and Heavens, some have gone forward so far that they have overcome the Dark power or "Negative to God" force; that they have learnt to do this by sticking to a few simple rules, or Commandments. Their lives have become Harmonious because they have found how to use their "Homeland" to its best advantage. There is no hunger, no poverty etc and all things are for everyone, not a precious few. He tells me that on an Earth like ours, same chemicals we mean, that they have for a long time sent to us pictures on a beam, some of these we call "Flying Saucers," but it is only the image we are seeing as its a picture of their form of travel, sent on a beam of high energy. Karaticus says its like when the Americans sent their message into Space, with details of our Earth.

Those Homelands nearer to us have sent many of their ships, not just in recent times, but long long ago as we are known for our destroying ways. We have destroyed our own air. They are worried that we will, if not checked, do much damage to the Earth which in turn will upset the balance of our part of the Galaxy.

The Middle Path

Beneath the surface of the Earth at this time many things are on the move preparing for the great upheaval that is on its way. Volcanoes are stirring, new ones are being formed, it is time we really shook off this apathy, and pulled ourselves together. How are we going to do it?

I have just asked Karaticus why he will insist that I keep my wording simple, and his reply is simple. We started off didn't we by saying that Man held God either too high or too low. Well, you are to take the Middle Path, not a lot of big words that complicate things. "God's message is Simple, Iah. Do unto others as you would like them to do unto you. Anything that's more complicated and you can't understand half of what is being discussed." He is quite right. If I don't understand something I lose interest! He says we are trying to show that the Middle Path in Life is the best way, if we don't care a damn then we are wrong. If we get too high and mighty we forget the reason for being so true to ourselves which is that in order to progress the Middle Path we need a clear conscience. It is no good reaping and sowing the same old thing time and time again. You have to learn from experience of life what is good and what is bad for you. So it's time for us all to wise up on this.

Let us take an instance; does gossip really upset you? Right! - so avoid it. And don't be afraid to voice that anger instead of standing and getting furious with someone who is making you angry with their gossip and you will find such a difference. if you turn and say quite plainly "I'm not interested!" you will feel come over you a very good feeling. Why? because the real you is happy that you have been true to yourself! Do your best to avoid situations that you really loathe and you will be much better for it because every time you get really agitated and angry you cut off the "self." It's as easy as that, you think only with the "Earthly Mind." Jesus Christ did this once when he became

74

so mad with the Money Lenders that he upturned the tables. While we are on this subject let me show you how Jesus overcame this. When he was dying he called out (with the Earthly Mind) "Father, why has thou deserted me?" Then his Spiritual Mind took over and he said "Not my will, but thy will be done." Do you see what I mean, when you have a problem, no matter what it is, let the Inner You be the guide. Try hard to keep a hold of yourself, just don't follow the crowd to be popular, you will be far more happy if you listen to the Inner Voice, the Middle Path. Do as God asks of you, Love Him, you don't have to bow and bob, just try very hard to listen to the good advice he has given you. Our advice is to read the *"instructions;"* ten of them, you don't need to read the whole history that's in his "Hand Book."

The next step is to try and follow them now you are not going to be Transfigured over night, but little by little you will find your outlook on life changing, simple things by doing and thinking so differently, into your mind will come a new way of thinking, and you will see life as it is! You will make plenty of mistakes. God has provided for this with the Redemption. If you feel that you are being tried in a situation beyond your power of standing then call out to your "Heavenly Father," and I promise you, you will get that help. Your faith is the link between Him and you. Recall to mind the Hymn "Oh God Our Help In Ages Past;" all through your many Lifetimes on this Earth he has always been there. We cannot see with our Earthly eyes but all around us are the "Givers of Protection and Light." Like a Television that has to be tuned in we also must tune ourselves in and Prayer goes out via the "Holy Ghost" (station) and like any Earthly Father, our "Heavenly Father" will send help to his "Children" in distress. We feel that Man has so been blinded by Man in the Scriptures, let us take the "Conception of Jesus Christ." This has been so blown up it has lost its meaning. It states "and the shadow of the most high shall overshadow you and you shall conceive a Son." There is no mystery, if you stand in the sun you cast a shadow, then if someone stands in front of you then your shadow is "over shadowed." What is known as the Immaculate conception is not only confined to the Holy Bible. It is in all Scriptures, it is to make the body less dense that this takes place then the Spirit housed in this body is on a more receptive plane of communication between the "Two Worlds" and is not so drawn down in the material world. It was in this state that Mary was able to conceive God's son, this is why it is told in the scripture at twelve years old Christ was left behind, while he was listening to the Wise Men. Why? because their words of knowledge drew him to them. Its not many lads of that age that want to hear words of wisdom is it? But you will see he was already to feed his soul with Spiritual nourishment. You will recall his words to his mum, "I am about my Fathers business." This couldn't have been Joseph, he was a Carpenter.

Karaticus says there is so much we could tell you about "Life Eternal" but we were called this time to show you that God is not dead, and that Man is starving our Spiritual bodies by being drawn down further and further into the material world and not preparing himself for the next step in his Progression, and we will have no-one but ourselves to blame for God has used many ways to warn Man. Both of us hope the very simple way we have tried to show you, of how to be very aware of *"Who You Are and Why You Are."* Will you make that extra effort to *Look Up* and *Walk Up The Middle Path*.

I am told by Karaticus it is time to rest, for a while to take a break from our work together, but we will return and bring more help in the future to show you "Gods ways are the only way and they are clear for all his Children to Understand."

I will go on in the way to which I was sealed in the cave in Crete. I hope my Gift will help many more sick brothers and sisters.

That my healing will as before help not only the sick in body but those whose minds are so full of distress they are making their bodies sick.

My brother Karatlcus and I, as I have said, are no strangers to each other. We have played many parts together, in this School of Learning, long ago, as I have shown, he really kept me steady when I was feeling so fed up with losing my way of life when the Temples were destroyed and I was stuck in a cave, he came to me then and held me up. He knew what was to take place, I didn't. I wasn't aware that I was to take on the "Seal" in the very near future, that was to be mine for all "Time."

I am more than aware now though, of what a wonderful "talent" has been given to me and I most sincerely pray I will at all times use it to the benefit of all who come to me for help.

Long ago, Jesus left the Earth, his mission complete. Now he expects us to follow him, I hope that if only one person is made to see with open eyes what we have tried to tell you, that Jesus will breathe a sigh of relief. Will that person be you?

Are you going to join my brother and I on the middle path? We hope so, when we depart this lifetime may we all meet in the Twilight Zone, or in the halls of learning.

The 2,000 years reign is drawing fast to a close. Please do not be so frightened of what Man can do with his destructive weapons, its the gods who control nature who will bring the cleansing. Use the energy you are using to fear in a new way and say to God "Thy will be done on earth as it is in heaven."

The Middle Path

Hold on tight to Faith for it can *"move mountains"* and those Mountains are your fear.

May the Gods of our Forefathers who are the same today, tomorrow and forever Bless you and stir your Minds to realise

WHO YOU ARE.